W9-CIP-786

ARE YOU LISTENING GOD?

(I need you)

ARE YOU LISTENING GOD?

(I need you)

**No frills prayers for the wounded &
the skeptical, for wobbly believers &
the spiritually fragile.**

❖

JOAN BEL GEDDES

Foreword by John Catoir

JOAN BEL GEDDES is the author of numerous books on subjects from child care to the civil rights movement. Her articles have apperared in many magazines and newsletters. She continues her freelance writing from her home in New York City and serves on the boards of several non-profit organizations.

© 1994 by Joan Bel Geddes

Are You Listening God was published in 1974 as *To Barbara With Love.*

All rights reserved. No part of this book may be used or reproduced in any manner whatsoever, except in the case of reprints in the context of reviews, without written permission of the publisher, Ave Maria Press, Inc., Notre Dame, IN 46556.

International Standard Book Number: 0-87793-533-5

Library of Congress Catalog Card Number: 94-71154

Cover and text design by Katherine Robinson Coleman

Cover photograph by Marilyn Nolt

Photography: Cleo Freelance Photo 68; Jean-Claude Lejeune 20, 42, 120, 154; Skjold Photographs 96.

Printed and bound in the United States of America.

Dedication

To Barbara *and* to Wink

Contents

FOREWORD

Every now and then an important book captivates me by its power and simplicity.

Joan Bel Geddes has written such a book. It is a beautiful series of prayers written for her sister Barbara Bel Geddes, the actress who played the mother in the long-running TV series, "Dallas." She wanted to help Barbara work through the tragic experience of her husband's long and painful death.

Barbara admitted she needed spiritual help during her husband's illness, but she lacked faith in God. She needed and wanted the strength to carry on day after day; Joan wanted to help her cope with the strain of it, especially the nights when the crushing tidal waves of worry, fear, grief, despair, and anger flooded over her. That was easier said than done.

One day, Barbara cried in exasperation, "Oh, if only I knew how to pray. If I had a prayerbook or something to help me. Joan, please try to get me one."

With that challenge, Joan began a search, but the initial enthusiasm turned to discouragement. After hunting through many bookstores and libraries for the right kind of prayerbook, she realized there was nothing available for the floundering believer. There were no books that started from the premise that the one praying is at best an agnostic.

When people are spiritually fragile, they do not feel comfortable with canned piety and none of the traditional prayerbooks dealt with that subtle problem. Neither could she find anything that took into consideration the doubts of a person who might be turned off by organized religion.

So Joan decided to write her own book of prayers tailored to her sister's need. She did this in a simple, straightforward series of prayers to help Barbara, but legions of good people like Barbara will also benefit from this labor of love.

The first chapter speculates about prayer and about faith. It is a cry of the heart. Here's an excerpt:

> (Oh God) I'm turning to you out of some kind of blind, primitive instinct, in a burst of hope against hope, a sort of reversion to childishness, even though I am not at all sure that you're there or that, if you are, you are powerful enough to help me or interested enough in me to want to help me. . . . Skepticism is like a high wall that keeps things from entering the mind, good ideas as well as bad—so I'm going to knock down that wall for a while, and invite in whatever thoughts want to come. My new "open door policy."

This is a good beginning because once the door of the mind is opened, all kinds of interesting thoughts and emotions are free to roam. The nonbeliever can suspend those nagging doubts that impede the heart from soaring to heaven.

Because this book was motivated by love, I feel the presence of the Holy Spirit who is Love on every page. Also the prayers are utterly honest, there are no frills or pretensions.

There's probably a little skepticism in every believer, and a little faith in every skeptic. The believer's skepticism is caused more by the imponderable truths of faith themselves than by an active suspension of assent. For instance, a true believer might ask, "How can there be three persons in one God?" or "How can Jesus be God and man at the same time?" or "Why does a good God permit evil?" These are not really doubts, they are merely an expression of the difficulties of a vibrant faith. Our minds are limited. "We see through a glass darkly," as St. Paul says.

Nevertheless, the believer says "yes" even though the propositions of faith are difficult if not impossible to comprehend fully.

Skeptics on the other hand withhold assent, and some of them become cynical in the process. And yet even they harbor the nagging question: "What if it is all true? After all, something doesn't come from nothing, and there is a whole universe out there. What if there is a God, hidden from view for some reason I don't understand? Maybe I'm wrong for trying to go it alone." And so it goes.

Joan Bel Geddes reached into her heart to minister to her sister during a difficult period of her life. And she did it superbly well. In the process I think she has also ministered to all of us.

John Catoir

Director of The Christophers

INTRODUCTION

The book you are looking at was, at first, designed to be read by only one person, my sister Barbara, at a time when she had a very special, very personal need for it. However, Barbara was convinced that many other people have the same need she had, so she asked me to share it by having it published, even though this meant having to expose her private pain. It was originally entitled *To Barbara With Love* but to make it clear that we hope its message will reach a great many more people, the title has been changed.

Barbara's husband was dying a long, lingering death. All day, every single day, for weeks that stretched into months, Barbara was staying at his side in a hospital room, hiding her agony, holding his hand gently, smiling at him, talking cheerfully to him—on the very slight chance that he might somehow know it and be a little bit comforted, even though he was in a deep coma. (Some of the doctors told her not to bother because it couldn't possibly do any good, but all the nurses said, "Good for you!" which shows that, although doctors may have more knowledge of medicine, nurses have more knowledge of the human heart. A priest I know said, "Her talking in case he is aware inside, her care, her devotion, is one of the most beautiful tributes to love, to person, and to trust—i.e., God—I have ever known.")

To find the strength she needed to keep on doing what she was doing day after day, and to try to find some peace at night when she was unable to sleep, she said to me one day, "How I wish I knew how to pray! Will you please get me a prayerbook?"

Barbara is a warm, active, enthusiastic person. She has spent most of her life busily relishing life, somewhat in the way the flowers and birds she loves so much do: blooming cheerfully and flying freely without stopping to wonder why. She has always been appreciative of God's gifts but not very curious about or attentive to their giver. When she used to say, "My God!" it was a vehement expletive to express joy or indignation, not a demonstration of piety (though I often suspect that God, being infinitely understanding, merciful, and resourceful, instantly and deftly translates such phrases, even—or especially—when they are uttered by self-proclaimed agnostics or atheists, recognizing them as implicit praise or disguised pleas for help, and responding with generosity).

She didn't have even an elementary Sunday School acquaintance with God. Having been a highly spirited little girl, she spent most Sunday mornings romping outdoors happily with a ball, a playmate, or a dog, while more decorous and docile little girls stayed in church singing hymns and memorizing prayers.

I proceeded to hunt in bookstores and libraries for a prayerbook for Barbara but couldn't find any that seemed appropriate or that were written in language I thought she would find appealing or even intelligible. They were all too theological, too dogmatic, too sentimental, too full of clichés, and they took for granted a foundation of religious faith which she simply didn't have. So the only thing I could think of to do—since I agreed with her that prayer might indeed help her—was to encourage her to take off on her own and, to get her started, I tried to put myself in her place and frame of mind and let a lot of thoughts and feelings tumble out onto paper, a mixture of bitter protests, puzzled queries, yearnings, and hopes.

Barbara read the book I wrote for her almost every day and used it, as I hoped she would, to go beyond it. She shared it with the nurses. With friends. With the hospital chaplain. With patients. With patients' families and visitors. She and the chaplain both urged me to publish it. The chaplain said, "You have no idea how many other people there are, especially in hospitals, who, like Barbara, could be helped by a book like this—people whose faith is weak, or nonexistent, or being tested more severely than they think they can bear."

Even devout believers, at certain times in their lives, find their faith wobbly, with fears and doubts threatening to annihilate it. Many of them add a feeling of guilt to their other torments, because they consider it sinful (as well as scary) to admit to any doubts about God. They think it pious and prudent to repress all doubts and pretend they don't exist.

However, in spiritual life doubts are a lot like weeds in a garden: when ignored, they may grow bigger and tougher and more abundant, instead of dying obligingly. And neglected weeds can end up by taking over and spoiling an entire garden.

On the other hand, if some weeds are boldly grasped and uprooted, while others are allowed to exist but kept in their place, a garden may be enhanced. Not all weeds (or doubts) are evil, by any means—daisies and asters, buttercups and day lilies are weeds, after all, and in the South Seas even orchids are. Instead of being a sign of weakness or wickedness, questions about the basis and implications of one's belief (or lack of belief) may be a sign of sincerity, intelligence, and growth. Doubts that are frankly faced and examined can lead to increased understanding and deepened humility. They may awaken and vivify, enrich and broaden faith rather than undermine it.

Faith is threatened by indifference and neglect, but not by honesty. And I don't think we should be ashamed to admit that we have more questions than answers. The essence and value of faith are not, it seems to me, to be found in confident dogmatic assertions and philosophical propositions but in the questing heart which seeks, desires, responds to, and reveres the highest good it is capable of knowing.

This book, therefore, faces real doubts and fears head on and asks a lot of searching, often "irreverent," questions. It takes as its starting point the assumption that the reader has no faith, and it never reaches a point of expecting complete acceptance of any specific creed or sect. It is meant merely to open a door on spiritual possibilities, rather than to lead the reader through the door. I do not believe anyone has the right or duty or power to decide for anyone else whether or not to walk through the door or how far to keep on walking.

Here, then, is Barbara's book—now yours. Not all of the speculations and reflections in it may apply to you. Some will undoubtedly seem more meaningful and relevant in certain situations and moods than at other times. But she and I offer the book to you in the hope that, whether you are a "believer" or a "nonbeliever," you will find a few thoughts on its pages which will "speak to your condition," as the Quakers say . . . not only in times of trouble and distress, when you feel confused and helpless, surrounded by thick darkness, but also at those other times—so hard to remember when one is unhappy—when the clouds scatter and the sun breaks through and the heart bursts with wonder at life's inexplicable but undeniable beauty.

Dear Barbara,

You said you wished you had a prayerbook, so I looked for one for you. But I couldn't find one I thought would be a real help to you.

Traditional prayerbooks use somewhat formal and old-fashioned language. Many are full of flowery phrases and *shalts* and *doths* and *vouchsafes* and *verilys* and *thees* and *thous*. You're not used to this vocabulary and it would seem stiff and artificial and distracting to you.

Also, most prayerbooks contain expressions of piety at its most fervent—sometimes expressing how people think they *ought* to feel rather than how they actually *do* feel—with passionate declarations of unquestioning faith, unwavering and deep devotion, and humility which would seem exaggerated and unreal to you. Or they speak of things you don't know much about, being based on a tradition and knowledge of religious doctrines (original sin, redemption and the cross, intercession, atonement, the Trinity, etc.) which would seem irrelevant to you and would confuse you rather than enlighten you.

Prayer, to be real and to be helpful, need not be eloquently and beautifully phrased—but it *must* be sincere. So a prayerbook that expresses yearnings and aspirations and convictions which are not yours can do more harm than good. Therefore I've tried to compose some prayers for you that are simple and honest and in modern language, that actually express "where you're at."

Please understand that I am not trying to put any thoughts or words into your head that don't apply to you. The words I've written are meant as suggestions, to be used as a springboard, just to start you off. Whenever you can or want to, substitute or add your own words (you'll find some of your own here already, anyway!). Don't think you have to read, or agree with, everything I've written. Just take a phrase here and there and if one of them leads you to think further along the lines it suggests, go to it in your own way. If it doesn't help, ignore it.

Don't be afraid to follow your thoughts wherever they carry you. You can't shock God, you can't bore God, and you can't seem ridiculous to God. You can cut yourself off from God if you're phony or ungrateful or unloving, but if you're sincere and wide open God's love will flow into you and over you and through you like the refreshing sweetness of a spring breeze in a garden after a rainstorm.

Don't try to force anything. But don't try to resist anything either. Just let yourself—and God—*be.*

Wing it!

Love,

Joan

1
God,
if you exist,
please
help me

PLEASE!

SOS   SOS   SOS

· · · — — · · ·   · · · — — · · ·   · · · — — · · ·

HELP!

DEAR GOD (if there is a God):

Please help me (if you can).

I need help but don't know where to find it.

If you exist, God, I apologize for ignoring you until now, and beg your forgiveness and help.

If you *don't* exist, I won't be any worse off for talking to Nothingness than I have been trying to maintain a heroic silence and independence.

I'm going to try to talk to you, God, and I'm going to try to get you to talk to me.

After all, why not gamble when there's nothing—except despair—to lose?

I'm turning to you out of some kind of blind, primitive instinct, in a burst of hope against hope, a sort of reversion to childishness . . . even though I am not at all sure that you're there or that, if you are, you are powerful enough to help me or interested enough in me to want to help me.

People are supposed to function with brains and education, not with blind instinct—but instinct serves animals and birds pretty well, and I've always said human beings are animals, so maybe I should trust this instinct.

I've always been skeptical—and I've always thought that skepticism was a virtue, a sign of sophistication and intelligence, because it protects people from believing in nonsense and superstition. It does, of course. But maybe it also "protects" people from believing in *true* things.

Skepticism is like a high wall that keeps things from entering the mind, good ideas as well as bad—so I'm going to knock down that wall for a while, and invite in whatever thoughts want to come. My new "open door policy."

It makes me feel awfully foolish—in fact, it's rather spooky!—to find myself trying to talk seriously to someone I'm not even sure is there.

However, if nobody is there then at least nobody will hear me making a fool of myself!

So I can forget about being embarrassed and just pour my heart out freely, hoping it will do some good. That's what I'm going to try to do.

Why have I always tried until now to be so independent, never asking God for help in coping with my problems (any more than I've thanked God when I didn't have any)?

I just assumed that God wasn't interested (or didn't exist) and that God would be no help even if I did turn to him. But I never tested this theory. Why?

Why was I so "unscientific"? It seems pretty rash to build a whole life on an untested hypothesis. And what made me think that my "unscientificness" and lack of curiosity were "smart"?

I've spent most of my life ignoring or turning away from God, and then considering the fact that I couldn't see God or hear God and knew nothing about God as evidence that God wasn't there.

I guess that's a bit like being blind and therefore concluding that color is nonexistent, or being deaf and therefore refusing to believe in the existence of music. Or like being illiterate and then taking that fact as proof that there's no such thing as literature.

It's not very logical. Rather unimaginative! Even a bit pigheaded?

Is it too late for me to change?

If there *is* a God who pays any personal attention to people, then God's probably mad at me, because I've never paid much attention to him—and I'm sure God's not very impressed with the fact that I have decided to at last, because I'm doing it as a result of my own personal (selfish?) need, not out of a sudden burst of true (unselfish) devotion. It seems rather rude and undignified to turn to someone for help if you have consistently ignored that someone until you needed help.

But people say that God is very forgiving, more forgiving than any human being would be, so I'll swallow my pride and ask God to let bygones be bygones.

Even if God exists, and can hear me, how do I know that God gives a damn? Come to think of it, if God doesn't exist God *can't* give a "damn" and that's some consolation, I guess . . .

I use that word "damn" so lightly! But it's really a very serious word. I've never believed in heaven (dismissing it as too good to be true) or hell (dismissing it as too bad to be true) or salvation or damnation, but I *have* learned that there are such things as "heavenly" happiness and "hellish" suffering. And I already *feel* damned, in a way, at least at moments, because I feel so damned lost and hopeless—and lost and hopeless are what the word "damned" means.

But I don't want to be lost and hopeless, and I'm *trying* to find guidance and purpose for my life, so I'm not a permanent failure ("a lost soul") yet! There is still a little bit of hope inside me. I'll try to cultivate it and make it grow, like a delicate little house plant.

I'm in front of you, God, like a newborn baby—defenseless and helpless and ignorant—screaming loudly and hungrily, without any tact, or clever strategy, or persuasive words, or bargaining devices.

I'm turning to you for help, not because I deserve it, or because I know how to get it, or because I expect it, but simply because I *need* it.

Help me if you can.

Please.

I'm ashamed of the fact that I feel so weak and helpless. Yet I suppose I really shouldn't be. There are times in almost everybody's life when things are so rough that you can't cope all by yourself. Trying to go it alone can result in a big mess and a full-blown nervous breakdown.

We get by with a little help from our friends, but it's not fair to burden friends *too* much with our problems (and there is a limit on how much most of them will let us, anyway). And a brilliant and sympathetic psychiatrist who will listen to our troubles isn't always available (besides, they are so expensive, and their help is so long-range).

So what can someone who needs help do? Turn to you? And actually get helped?

I wonder . . . I doubt . . . but I hope . . .

I think I'm just babbling to myself—like a lonesome kid who invents an Imaginary Friend.

But other people talk to you, God, and lots of them think they even get answers. **So** I'm going to keep trying.

If something is potentially worthwhile, one shouldn't give up too easily.

I have no genuine conviction that there is a God who is really personally interested in any individuals, including me. I am only one among how many billions and zillions of people, after all, so how could the maker and ruler of the cosmos be interested in, or even aware of, me? I'm like a mere grain of sand on a huge beach, so it's pretty hard to believe I'm of much importance to anyone except myself and a few other people.

Still, I know there are many people who are convinced that God actually knows them and loves them and looks after them individually. If them, then why not me too? Maybe they know something I don't.

If God is so clever, I suppose God must be able to attend to little things as well as big ones.

I can't get rid of my doubt, but I'm going to give God—at least temporarily—"the benefit of the doubt" and see what happens.

I'm so low right now that I have no place to go but up.

So I'm reaching *up*.

2
Reaching
out
for
God

How shall I go about this?

What I'm *not* going to do is try to impress God—or myself—by trying to compose poetic prayers or pious essays. I'm not hoping to get an A in English Composition.

I'm not even going to try to think such profound and beautiful thoughts that I could get an A in a philosophy course.

I'm going to try simply to be ME—the most honest, sincere, open-minded, open-hearted me I can be.

And then I'm going to try, with as little affectation and prejudice as possible, to see what—if anything—I can discover about me *and* about YOU *and* about the relationship between us.

I want to try to reach outside myself, way, way up and far, far out, beyond all the agitation and confusion and disappointment and pain of life, to see if I can somehow get to understand the Heart and Soul of the universe . . . and I'm also going to try to dig way, way down into the untapped depths of myself, below all my worries and fears and complaints and bewilderment, to see if I can unlock a door so that my heart and soul can get some badly needed fresh air.

I want to learn to understand myself better than I do, to know more about *what* and *why* and *who* and *where* I am. And I also want to see if I can understand life itself better than I do, to see if I can make any real sense out of what it's all about.

I'm not very philosophical or religious or pious by nature. I find it very hard (and boring) to concentrate on abstract ideas, so I have always left philosophy to professional philosophers and religion to priests and nuns (figuring they had some neurotic reasons to be obsessed with God instead of living "normal" lives like the rest of us). Now I suddenly wish I had the philosopher's wisdom or the religious person's faith, to help see me through stormy times and to give me strength to face tragedy without despair—but I don't know how to acquire it.

Is there any way you can help me find you, God, if you *do* exist? And if you do, can you really help me to be a stronger and better and happier person than I am?

Please do whatever you can!

Maybe prayer is just a sort of self-hypnosis. You're not actually talking to anyone except yourself but you convince yourself that you are. However, I suppose that, if the things you say to yourself are constructive, it can still be a useful procedure.

But I really do hope that I'm talking to Somebody other than just myself, because I'm looking for a source of strength and understanding that is much, much greater than any I possess on my own.

I say I want to believe in a good God, but the second I find myself starting to be at all receptive to such a belief I also find myself fighting it off! I wonder why I am so reluctant to believe something that I think I would like to believe.

Afraid of being wrong? Afraid of being silly? But it's just as wrong and silly to refuse to believe something that is true as it is to believe something that is not true.

The trouble is: How do you find out which is which?

Help me to remember that, even though some believers are crackpots, not *all* of them are stupid or insane. Many of them, in fact, are far more intelligent and better educated and saner than I am! So don't let me dismiss their views as utterly absurd.

Is hoping one form of praying? If so, maybe I've already begun to learn how to pray!

Is my reaching out for a God that I could get to know and love and trust a prelude to faith, or the actual first step in faith? I long to believe in and to get to know and love and count on God the way a thirsty soldier lost in a desert longs to find, and to drink, and to be refreshed by water! If I keep searching for God will I discover God (or only a mirage)?

If "desire for" is the same thing as "love" then perhaps I already *do* love God!

(How about that? My lifelong skepticism must have been pretty superficial! If I put some "faith" in its place I hope it won't be equally superficial.)

Faith is just a "crutch," I've always said, rather sneeringly. But why sneer at crutches? When someone breaks a leg a crutch is a very useful thing! It wouldn't make sense to refuse to avail yourself of a crutch when you needed a crutch. That would be self-destructive pride, rather than intelligent independence.

Another thing about crutches: If they weren't made of real wood or metal they wouldn't do any good. An *imaginary* crutch would be almost as useless as *no* crutch. So if faith really *does* help people, that must mean they're leaning on something that actually does exist. Something *real*, something solid, must support them.

What makes people who have faith in God sure they are placing their faith in something real and reliable? How do they know (or don't they) that they're not deluded?

Well, when someone tells me something, how do I decide whether I believe him or not? I judge by what I think about that person's reliability. I believe him if I want to, if I trust him, if I respect him, if I love him. I *choose* to believe (or not) and then I *act* upon that choice (and then, later on, I find out by the results whether my faith or distrust was justified or misplaced).

Shall I take a bold leap in the dark and place some faith in God—*act* as if I were sure of God even though I'm not— and then see what the result is?

Surely it isn't the most sensible tactic, when you want favors from someone, to keep telling him you doubt that he's smart enough or nice enough to give you what you're asking for! Instead of arguing with and acting suspicious of God, I should probably try to flatter God and get on God's good side . . . on the other hand, that wouldn't do any good, actually, because they say God can read our hearts and knows all of our hidden secrets. So if I pretended to have more faith and love and hope than I actually do have, God would know perfectly well that I was faking.

That kind of phony prayer would be useless. That really would be self-delusion, as distinguished from *real* prayer. (Hmmm? Have I reached the conclusion that real prayer is *not* self-delusion? Maybe I'm beginning to understand something important!)

If it's true that God hates hypocrisy more than God hates almost anything, then it's good that I am being honest with God and not giving "false worship." You can't honor Truth with lies.

Faith and hope and love are triplets—they grow together. If one weakens, they all do. If one gains strength, they all do. The important thing, I guess, is not to misplace them, by loving and believing in and relying on "false gods" instead of a (or the?) real one.

But how can I make sure that I won't worship a false god? One way, I suppose, is for me to be thoroughly real and true, as *un*false, myself, as I know how to be. I truly want to hunt for Truth—unevasively, unprejudicedly, untimidly, unambiguously, honestly—and I want to commit myself to accepting and respecting whatever Truth I can discover and recognize.

I am looking for comfort and consolation, yes, but not for *false* comfort or consolation based on pretense and delusion. One of the definitions of the God I'm looking for is "Truth." I want to believe only in whatever-there-is-that-is-truly-true.

I think I'll draw up a "Help Wanted" ad:

Faith Needed. Honest-to-God variety, guaranteed to soothe pains, strengthen courage, increase hope, and cure ills. Need large enough supply to last several months. Would prefer lifetime supply and guarantee but will consider temporary loan. Please describe fully, with details about size, brand, cost, and where it can be obtained.

What *is* faith? Here I am wishing I had some, trying to acquire some, and I'm not even sure just what it is!

People who say they have "faith in God" are saying not only that they believe God exists but that God is good and looks after them. But do they mean that they *know* this, or just that they *think* it and *hope* it's true?

When I see a chair I don't have "faith" that it is there—I *see* it and *know* it's there. And when it's raining I don't simply "believe" that it's raining—I *know* it is. So faith isn't quite the same thing as knowing-for-sure, is it?

Having faith doesn't mean knowing something about which you have undeniable and tangible proof. Yet it must be more than just guessing or wishing, because it's definite enough to comfort and inspire people. And some people have been so deeply convinced of their faith that they have actually been willing to die for it. Or to live by it—which may be even harder!

Knowing that a chair is here is simple recognition of a fact, not faith. But if I decided I was willing to sit on the chair, trusting it wouldn't collapse under me, that would be placing faith in it.

And seeing it rain isn't faith—but if I thought about the rain and about the fact that it has the amazing power to refresh the earth and to make life and growth possible, irrigating crops and providing food and drink, and if I decided to use the rain water to drink or to bathe, then I'd be exercising faith in its ability to refresh and cleanse me.

In short, just knowing a fact that has been proved is simply common sense; you *have* to accept it or be crazy. But faith, I guess, is a kind of *un*common sense, involving a voluntary assent: cooperation with, and gratitude for, and constructive use of the facts that you think you know.

Faith is an *attitude* one takes about what one thinks one knows. It isn't a synonym for knowledge, yet it doesn't mean *less* than knowledge. It's different, and in a way *more* than, because it has added ingredients: free will and commitment.

In other words, faith is active, not passive; voluntary, not compulsory; positive, not neutral. It involves the will and the heart, not just the brain.

So please, God, strengthen my will and warm my heart as well as enlightening my mind— if you can, and if I will let you. I'll try. Will you too, please?

It's irrational (in fact, it can be disastrous) to place faith in what a person tells you if that person doesn't know what he is talking about or is a liar. When you want to learn about something, you don't ask someone who knows nothing about it or who would deliberately mislead you. Probably the best source of information about something would be its inventor or manufacturer (if he's honest!). So the Maker of life ought to know more and be able to tell me more about what life is all about, and what it is for, than anyone else—if that Maker can be contacted.

When I was first created I trusted my creator implicitly without any effort: I slept peacefully, smiled and gurgled cheerfully, yelled expectantly whenever I needed something. That was pretty sensible of me . . . surely, if you can trust *anyone*, you ought to be able to trust your own creator!

Now that I'm older I think I am going to have to learn to do consciously what I did then *un*consciously.

Having faith in one's creator means relying on, trusting, and respecting (i.e., loving?) something or someone that is much more powerful, much greater, than oneself—or at the very least, something very different from oneself.

Well, if God knows how to create solar systems and keep them running, and can turn tadpoles into frogs, and wriggly caterpillars into soaring butterflies, and infinitesimal eggs and sperm into human beings, it's quite clear that God knows a lot more than I do! So it might be sensible for me to place myself in God's hands and trust God more than I do.

A flower accepts what the gardener does to and for it, without understanding him or it, just as a baby trusts and loves its parents and life, without being able to follow grown-up conversations or getting any explanation of how and why he is here. Is that more evidence that faith involves something different from mere knowledge, something more, something extra: acceptance, respect, and peaceful trust?

I guess faith isn't a word that means "the ability to understand and know for sure all about an unfathomable mystery" (life or God) but a word that means "the willingness to *respect* mystery and to *accept* it and *cooperate* with it, whatever-it-is."

Even if I can never hope to understand everything, maybe I can focus on a few important points and understand *something*. You don't have to study and memorize and check the accuracy of an entire world atlas to find out that Boston is in Massachusetts.

If I can learn about, and become convinced of, a few main points about God, then perhaps I can peacefully accept other things about God on faith.

Once again, I guess that's what is meant by "faith": accepting something, even when you cannot entirely understand it or prove it, simply because you think that someone else who understands more than you do is *trustworthy*. You do your best to pick a reliable doctor and then you place yourself in his hands, showing faith in him when you're sick and want to get well . . . you pick a reliable airline and then trust the pilot to get you where you want to go instead of thinking that you have to learn how to fly the airplane by yourself.

Where can I find a trustworthy guide who can help me fly to God?

I wish I were *sure*, God, that you love me and everyone else you have made, and that you are always looking out for each of us and guiding us toward what is good for us, but I don't really, truly, fully believe it—because it's too good to be true!

On the other hand, I can't believe that you *definitely* don't love your own creation and don't know how to lead it where you want it to go. Why would you bother to create things if you didn't love them? And shouldn't you know *why* you made them and what is the best thing to do with them, if you're smart enough to know how to make them in the first place?

I wonder what it would take to make me really believe in God's love for me? A miracle? I'd probably explain it away!

If I prayed for something and didn't get it I'd consider that proof (strong evidence, anyway) that God doesn't exist or at least doesn't answer prayer. But if I prayed for something and then *did* get it, I bet I'd think it was just a lucky coincidence.

That's sort of an unfair double standard, isn't it? With that attitude on my part, no matter what God does—whether God answers my prayers or not—God can't win. (Nor can I!)

I'm afraid I'm pretty stubborn and hard to convince. And if I'm *that* hard to convince, I don't see how even Omnipotence can get through to me.

Am I fighting against God and also against my own best interest?

I can't *make* myself believe something just because I'd *like* to believe it, or because other people do—but help me at least to be *willing* to believe good things, instead of putting up mental barricades against them and saying, "It's too good to be true."

Lots of things in this world would seem "too good to be true" if we had never seen them or experienced them so that we *know* they're true:

> Springtime.
> Sunsets.
> Babies.
> Orgasms.
> Roses.
> Music.
> Food when you're hungry.
> Drink when you're thirsty.

(I wonder if that's why bread and wine are appropriate signs of God's existence and presence and care for us.)

Anyone who has ever been in love with someone and whose love has been wonderfully returned *knows* that something too good to be true *can* be true! So perhaps it's not totally absurd to think that each of us can love God *and* that God can love each of us—especially if love is God's very nature . . .

But does God?

And is it?

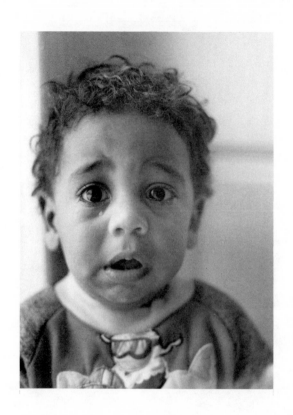

3
Trying
to accept
the existence
of pain
and suffering

Oh God, everything is so confusing and tangled!

Reality keeps getting in the way of my efforts to understand and accept Reality! I try to be hopeful and patient and philosophical about things, but then I look around me and see so many frightful things that I just *cannot* accept. The world is so full of hate and misery and ugliness and evil, and yet religious people say you are loving and you made it and are guiding it!

I *wish* I could understand it—and them—and you, God!

If you really exist and you care about individuals, including me, then how come you have let me reach the point where I am so unhappy and frightened and confused that I need to cry out for help? Why didn't you help me sooner?

In other words, God—if you can hear me—if you really like me at all, then why haven't you taken better care of me? And how can anyone think you are Perfect and All Powerful and Loving when you let people have such a hard time?

If I were God I'm sure I wouldn't let people suffer as much as you let them. Am I better, more generous and kinder, than you are? How can I worship a God who is less kind than I am?

That's not a flippant question. I'm dead serious. Why and how do so many people believe in you and love you even when their lives are full of pain and disappointment?

It's so hard for me to approach you politely and "reverently" and to say "Thank you, God" for the good things in life, when right now I am so much more aware of bad and sad things. Right now everything looks so bleak and black to me that I can hardly even remember blue sky and sunshine and babies' smiles and the beauty of a loving kiss. I really don't feel very grateful to you today. Instead, I feel hurt, and confused, and angry, and scared, and resentful!

I don't see why I should have to suffer so much. I suppose that sounds selfish of me. Other people suffer, so why should I be immune? But I don't see why *anybody* has to suffer! *Why* is life so hard, and why should I be grateful to a creator who lets it be so hard?

When I think about this I get so mad at you, God!

But how can I be mad at someone unless that someone exists? So, is my protest against the way God does things actually some kind of "act of faith"? Do I have a sort of built-in (God-given) sense of justice that he gave me, that is a small reflection of his own justice? Is there actually "justice" in the universe, to which my heart intuitively responds and for which it longs, but which operates in such a complex way that I can't always see and understand it?

In some strange way I must trust God more than I realize, because I have the nerve to ask him to pay attention to me and to help me when I've never paid attention to or done anything for him. I must really believe that God's pretty generous—loving, in fact—even though I keep saying I don't and can't.

God will *have* to be generous to be willing to help me when I keep accusing him of neglect or injustice—especially when it's really, to such a large extent, the other way around, because I have been neglectful of (and unjust to?) God! I say I want to pray to God, but most of my "praying" is challenging and arguing and insulting God! Complaining about the way God treats people and even telling God that he's not "all there."

Be generous and forgiving, God . . . and teach *me* to be generous and forgiving too.

Again and again I keep coming back to the same basic question. I can't help feeling rebellious and wondering why there is such a thing as suffering, if God is both powerful and good.

Well, let me see if I can get a glimmer of understanding by thinking about some things I know of which are both good and powerful in themselves yet which sometimes result in people's suffering . . . for instance, money—fame—family relationships—the telephone—automobiles—or . . .

The law of gravity is a good thing. It's necessary to hold me (and everything else) to the earth. But if I defy or ignore it, I will fall down and get hurt, as a direct result of this good law. Should I blame gravity for my hurt (like a child who sobs "mean old floor")?

Arithmetic is a good thing. As a result of it, I can keep track of things and construct and obtain and measure things that are useful. But if I make a mistake in arithmetic I will lose money or my clothes won't fit or something. That would be *my* fault, though, not arithmetic's.

Weather is a good thing. It provides the world with the sun and rain and air (and hence food) that we couldn't live without. It can cause floods and hurricanes and colds in the nose and sunburn, but it's still a good thing. We have to invent houses and dams and reservoirs and umbrellas and sweaters to cope with it; we have to accept it and learn to cooperate intelligently with it. If we fail to we suffer, but that's *our* fault, not the fault of the rain, the wind, or the sun.

Maybe "God's law" is a sort of super law of gravity, or arithmetic, or weather system. We suffer if we defy it or are unobservant of it, not because God is being mean but because we are being ignorant or foolish. But we don't like to admit stupidity, so we pass the buck and blame God instead of ourselves.

I've never felt the desire or need to figure out a philosophy or religion before. Is that one of the reasons God allows us to have trouble, because they make us look for help, and therefore for God, and finding out about God is the most important thing we can do and the only sure way we can find out what we are all about?

It seems a pretty drastic way to go about things, rather ruthless!

But how else can God get the attention of people like me who consistently ignore him? And if it's important for our welfare for us to get close to God, then maybe God *has* to be "ruthless," like a parent who disciplines instead of ignoring it when his children run wild, being "cruel in order to be kind."

The question, "Why is there such a thing as evil?" is really much too big a question for any one answer to explain. There are so many different kinds of evil—*physical* (pain, sickness); *emotional* (sorrow, fear, anger); *moral* and *spiritual* (selfishness, crime, sin)—and each of them, and each example of each of them, has different causes.

Some evils are simply due to the fact that we are finite creatures living in a still unfinished, evolving world. The limitations on our understanding and abilities make us suffer. For example: the diseases we haven't yet learned to conquer, and the injustices we haven't yet learned (or firmly enough decided) to prevent. Those are challenges we haven't yet surmounted. But as humanity (both the individual human being and the human race as a whole) grows and becomes wiser, such evils can be diminished, even abolished. (*Can* be but might not be—because we are free to do things or not do things and evils can't be abolished unless people are willing to do what is necessary to abolish them.)

Our love and our knowledge are still very incomplete, but maybe that isn't the fault of love or knowledge (in short, God's fault). Love and knowledge must be *discovered, appreciated, understood,* and *applied* before happiness can be complete.

Maybe that's why we're here: to learn to do that.

If people didn't eat anything they would die of starvation. And if they didn't drink anything they would die of thirst. In neither case would it be fair or accurate to say that food and drink had caused their suffering—it would be *lack* of food and drink that had done it.

In the same way, if God (creative goodness and love and truth and beauty) is nourishing food and drink for people's hungry and thirsty souls, then they will be spiritually healthy (hence happy) if they receive God, and spiritually starved and ill (hence wretched) if they don't . . . but if they don't, do they have any right to blame God for their misery?

Many people are not actually starving but are nonetheless malnourished. They eat too little, or they eat and drink the wrong kinds of things, so they get sick. When they do, it is their fault (though perhaps not intentionally), not the fault of food, agriculture, nature, farms, farmers, cattle ranchers, grocers, delicatessens, pharmacies, doctors, cooks, dietitians, medicine, etc.

In the same way, when we do things that make ourselves or other people unhappy, perhaps it's our fault, not life's or God's. If we want to be happy we have to learn to do and use the *right* things in the *right* way, not inappropriate or unneeded things in an unfitting or useless way.

From personal experience I know (though I wish I didn't!) that we human beings create many of our own woes, or at least make those we have far worse than they need be. How many times have I suffered (and made other people suffer too) because of what I did, rather than because of what someone else, or a cruel fate, or "God," did?

So often I've been lazy and selfish, thus making some simple task twice as hard as it would have been otherwise. Or I have been cowardly and suspicious, and my fears have made the thing I dreaded much more horrifying than it really was. Or I have been cross, even nasty, and have spoiled not only my day, but someone else's too. I've lost my temper so often (even with the people I love most in the world, my own family, and oh how I wish I could take it back!) and have thereby turned minor difficulties and disagreements into big, serious, bitter quarrels—and then I've been too proud or stubborn to apologize or to forgive, thus prolonging and deepening hurts which could have ended quickly.

If I'm honest and realistic, I guess I must admit that it's not necessary to search very far to find the explanation of some of the evils that have hurt me the most seriously. They weren't caused by an inconsiderate God. They were caused by *me*!

Some people produce suffering (their own and/or other people's) by intentionally and deliberately cheating or hurting other people. That's what "sin" is, I suppose. I hate that word "sin" because so many bluenoses tend to call everything that's any fun sin, and because so many proud and hardhearted people condemn other people for "sins" they can't help—wrong actions that are due to weakness or ignorance or problems they don't know how to handle. But I guess there really is such a thing as sin (and being bluenosed and proud and hardhearted may qualify! Some of the harsh sin-condemners may be unwittingly condemning themselves).

In other words, sinners are to blame for the existence of sin, I guess—not God! But why does God *allow* sinners to commit sins and thus to produce unhappiness and injustice, if God is "all-powerful" and therefore could prevent it?

Is the reason God allows sin and other evils to exist because God is a permissive teacher or guiding spirit rather than a dictatorial czar?

From God's infinite supply of power and love does he give to each of us a small amount of power and love and then leave the way in which we use these gifts up to us? And if we happen to use them unwisely, incorrectly, we then have to accept the unpleasant results of what we've done?

When we use power or love or freedom unwisely we are making an error, a wrong choice. And the result of something wrong is (logically enough!) something wrong—i.e., evil.

Is life a game of "Truth or Consequences"?

Perhaps God is more interested in having us learn how to use, intelligently and creatively, the freedom and knowledge we are given than God is in protecting us from our errors. (When a parent or teacher is unwilling to let children risk failure he prevents them from ever doing anything important on their own.)

Freedom and power and knowledge are glorious things, but dangerous, too. They can be misused. They entail risks. Are they worth the risks involved? God seems to think so! Certainly people who have been deprived of them think so. Anyway, *everything* worth doing involves the willingness to take risks and the real possibility of failure. Even babies, as they take their first steps, have to be brave enough to accept the possibility that they may fall down and hurt themselves, or they would never learn to walk.

Please give me the courage I need, God. And stamina. And perseverance.

Almost all of us love some things too little and other things too much and, as a result, we hurt ourselves or each other. For example:

If I love calorie-filled chocolate cake too much more than I love vitamin-filled celery I may hurt myself by becoming too fat. If I love money too much more than I love honesty I may hurt myself and someone else by becoming a thief. A bigot loves people too little. A tyrant loves power too much. A mugger loves excitement and violence more than he loves the welfare of his neighbor.

In other words, when we love anything excessively or insufficiently, we cause harm. But why, God, do you let us do that? Why don't you *stop* us when we are about to misuse your gifts?

Well, I suppose you can't abolish food every time someone is about to overeat, or suspend the law of gravity every time someone is about to fall down! If you always prevented us from making mistakes, or always rescued us from the consequences of our mistakes, you'd be like an overprotective mother and we'd never learn the right way to do things. And maybe that's what life is all about: If we want the world to be a happy place, and we want to have a "good" time here, we have to learn to love and to use appropriately the "good" things of life, the right things, goodness.

Perhaps God is like the author and/or director of a play, with a creative concept the actors are meant to study and develop, but after he leaves them on their own on opening night they forget about the original intention and betray it because they are so busy with their own petty egotistical concerns. Once "Daddy" (or "God"), the creator, has launched the play and left the cast to perform on its own, individual selfishness crops up. The actors don't care about the writer's purpose and forget the director's instructions—everything becomes me, me, me, with each person out for him or herself instead of caring about the rest. They distort and destroy what they are meant to build together.

To do whatever one can to maintain faithfully an author's creative concept is a real challenge for actors during a long run. So often when they think they are being inventive and original they are simply spoiling things, ruining the original idea, inspiration, energy, rhythm, and taking things out of proportion because they are bored or self-centered.

That may be a good comparison with what happens offstage too. We mess up our Author's original intention and creation through our false values, vanity, and incompetence.

But *some* evils are *not* our fault! Babies born with terrible congenital defects, for instance. Earthquakes. Famines. People cut down in their prime by frightful, painful diseases. You are to blame for *those* awful things, aren't you, God?

Nature is, anyway, because nature is an impersonal set of forces which is both creative and destructive, kind and cruel, beautiful and hideous. (Yet I *love* nature! The same life force that makes a cancer grow also makes flowers and babies grow. The same power that pushes a devastating hurricane also propels a gentle breeze. The same force that makes volcanoes erupt and kill people forms beautiful islands and mountains.)

This very awesome, baffling, magnificent nature—or God, its author—gives us terrible problems but *also* gives us brains and wills so that we can learn to *solve* problems and to control and change nature itself. So we are to blame when we waste our brains, time, and money, as we all too often do, acquiring unnecessary possessions or building expensive weapons with which to kill people instead of using our brains, time, and money to produce the constructive things that all of us need so badly, like medical research, hospitals, and schools.

We have to keep on trying to learn more and more and more, to cope better and better and better, to make fewer and fewer mistakes. We're not meant to collapse and give up when we face difficulties. Conquering problems may involve devastatingly hard work, but it can be awfully exhilarating too.

Helen Keller showed how one can use the powers God gives us, even when these are very, very limited, to surmount our problems if we will work at it instead of feeling sorry for ourselves and wasting our energy and time in bitter and futile complaints. Faith and courage can transform even great tragedies into great triumphs.

Some suffering comes from our *ignorance* of reality and some comes from our *resistance* to reality. In nature, each creature, whether it knows it or not, serves a larger purpose than its own existence (like plants and animals that provide food). If each of us could realize and accept this, and learn to do consciously and purposefully what we are meant to do, we would certainly suffer much less than we do. It's like childbirth: A woman who is fearful or resentful resists the contractions and experiences them as excruciatingly painful, while a relaxed woman who welcomes them finds childbirth quite bearable and can even feel comfortable and thrilled during it.

If we could all learn to do everything that we should do or have to do *willingly* we wouldn't mind doing it—by definition.

God, teach me not to resist and resent (and thus increase the pain of) the demands life makes on me.

Instead of asking why there is such a thing as unhappiness, perhaps there is an even more fundamental question I should ask:

Why is there such a thing as happiness?

After all, *un* just means *non*, and it is really far more remarkable that something wonderful should exist than that it should be nonexistent.

However, we seem to be made in such a way that we *expect* happiness. We are shocked and angry when we lose it, instead of being absolutely amazed when we find it. Somehow, we must think—even the most cynical of us—that this is basically meant to be a good and pleasant world and that evil is a distortion of and blot upon it, rather than thinking this is basically an evil world and that goodness and happiness are inexplicable, unexpected perversions.

So perhaps goodness and happiness are actually more basic, reliable, and frequent things than evil and sorrow ... even though one doesn't feel as if that's true when one is hurting.

When things have gone right for me I haven't usually given God any credit for it. I've praised nature, or "luck," or myself, or my friends, or associates, for the things I love that have made me happy—or I've simply taken them for granted without bothering to say "Thank you" to anybody or Anybody.

On the other hand, so often, when things have gone wrong, I've laid the blame at your door, God. I've complained about hardships and injustice and pain and have blamed everything bad that happens in the world on you. Yet at the same time I've said that disease and cruelty and suffering prove there isn't any God. Somehow it has rarely seemed to occur to me, when I've seen evidence of beauty and goodness and health and happiness, that *those* things might be proof that there *is* one.

I've been inconsistent, I guess, as well as ungrateful.

I'm sorry.

Does it make sense to blame Goodness for badness? Or Beauty for ugliness? Or Love for hatred? Or Truth for errors?

If God is Goodness and Beauty and Love and Truth, then evil is God's *opposite*, not one of God's attributes. It exists when God is ignored or defied, not when God is revered and obeyed. It's proof of how terribly ugly, how ghastly, how sad the world would be if there were no such things as Truth or Beauty or Goodness or Love, no God.

Evils are signs that we can use to remind us of how much we ought to appreciate, relish, revere, reciprocate, and love Goodness, Truth, Beauty, and Love!

I'm not going to adopt Pollyanna as a patron saint and pretend that I accept the existence of evil, suffering, and pain as if I don't really mind them, or as if I fully understand why they are part of human life. I am *not* happy about unhappiness!

But then, we're not actually supposed to *accept* such things, in the sense of thinking they don't matter, are we? We're supposed to mind evil enough to try to get rid of it, to fight it and conquer it with its opposite: goodness . . . learning to replace ignorance with knowledge, foolishness with wisdom, illness with health, sorrow with joy, selfishness with generosity, cruelty with kindness, war with peace, despair with hope, doubt with faith, hatred with love.

I'll try to be one of the people who try.

4
Thinking about the meaning *if any* of life and death

If most of our sufferings result from human ignorance and mistakes which God allows us to make—in the same way that a good parent or teacher allows children to make mistakes because personal experimentation and experience and observation are the best or only means by which people can truly discover and fully understand the things they are meant to learn—that might make good sense, except for one thing. We so often learn what we need to know too late!

What's the point of learning how to live happily and constructively if life ends as soon as we have learned that? If this life is all we have, then the way we learn-through-suffering is a somewhat ridiculous exercise in futility.

But *is* this all there is? Or is life a preliminary to something else? Is this earth a place of preparation rather than of fulfillment? Dress rehearsal rather than opening night?

Has life really got any purpose, and permanent value? Or is it just a sadistic joke? A pointless accident? A temporary problem? A tale full of sound and fury, signifying nothing? Or is there a good explanation for all the things in life that distress and confuse us, which some day we will be able to understand, even though we can't now?

Oh God, what's the point of my asking you all these questions? I feel as if I'm talking to an uninterested deaf-mute!

Can you hear me? Are you paying any attention to me? Can, and if so will, you respond to me and answer me? How? When?

I don't expect to hear voices or see visions—so how will you get through to me? By putting thoughts in my head if I'll shut up long enough to let you?

I long to believe that there is a good and lasting purpose to my life, and to all life, and that whatever and whoever is good will endure instead of being wiped out in pointless oblivion.

Obviously, most people (including me) must unconsciously and instinctively believe this, or we wouldn't work as hard as we do to accomplish difficult tasks and achieve long-range goals—often at great sacrifice—striving to develop our talents, to plan and build for the future, to create enduring works of art, to raise families, or to do anything that takes a lot of effort. We would just drift—unconcerned, hopelessly, aimlessly.

Life is so scary in so many ways. And so sad. And growth is so painful. Teething babies, bewildered adolescents, women in labor, ill and aging people staring into death (and trying to pretend they don't notice it)—all of these are so frightened. As am I.

But out of the baby's sore gums come strong teeth, with which the baby smiles happily and beautifully and can eat nourishing food.

The adolescent matures more, and becomes freer, more competent.

The woman in labor produces a miracle: another human being, more interesting and sweeter than anything she could have imagined.

Perhaps the frightened older or sick person is struggling painfully but fruitfully too, in a process of growth— toward something unknown. Perhaps what we see as physical decay and death are like pruning or molting or hibernating: transformation, rather than destruction. Viewpoints are so relative: Depending on where one is, another person is leaving or arriving, going up or coming down, dying or being born.

Many people believe that this life we now know is not the whole story, but just its *preface*: Act One of a drama, rather than Acts One, Two, and Three. Between the time when the curtain rises and when it falls we do learn an awful lot—partly voluntarily, through observation and study; partly involuntarily, through exposure and suffering. Do we really ever get a chance to use what we've learned—or is it wasted?

If this world is a rehearsal studio or a training school, then the sufferings we go through and the learning we acquire are *not* pointless. But that's a big *if* ! And wouldn't the actors or pupils be told?

Well, not necessarily. The baby in the womb is actually being prepared for another life, but doesn't realize it. (And maybe we *have* been told but I just haven't been listening! Christians think this is precisely why Christ was sent into the world, to bring us this "good news," and many other religious leaders have brought the same message in different words.)

Everyone seems to feel "immortal longings"—some kind of inborn hope or belief that there is something on the other side of every mountain, and on the unseen opposite shore of every lake and ocean, and out beyond the farthest star our eyes can see, beyond every obstacle, every path, every horizon, every limitation.

This strange mixture of faith in, and hope for, and love of, eternal life is every bit as characteristic of human beings as eyes, noses, legs, and arms are. *Those* parts of us are adapted to reality. They are useful. Could *this* so-basic part of us be the one exception to the rule, and be utterly, uniquely useless?

How could our deepest, most serious quality be the height of foolishness?

Can any inborn, universal aspiration be entirely baseless? Isn't a strong desire for something always inspired by that something's qualities, so that the desire couldn't exist unless the "something" also did?

Babies yearn for food—because they need it.
And it exists.
Artists yearn for beauty—they need it.
And it exists.
Everyone yearns for love—we all need it.
And it does exist.

Would it actually be possible for our minds to think of and our hearts to desire something that didn't in any way exist? We don't go around wishing we had sixteen legs, because we know humans are "meant" to have just two. People used to long to fly before they knew how, but if there were no such thing as flying they would never have thought of it.

Do people hope for an afterlife because there is something in us that *is* eternal? So that we have some kind of true instinct, by which we realize that we are heading for somewhere else? The way geese "know" they are going to go south in the winter, even when they have never been there and can't read maps or road signs?

Before I was born I could never possibly have conceived of this world. Someone or something with far, far greater power and knowledge about life processes than I have brought me (and everything else that's here) into this world.

My previous life was a true and fitting preparation for this life, even though it gave me no knowledge about, or understanding of, or belief in that fact. I was *pushed* out of the womb, which was then the entire known universe as far as I was concerned—unwittingly, involuntarily, protesting vigorously—into a new and unknown-to-me world. Yet I have discovered since then that this world I now live in is not only real, but *much* more interesting, varied, beautiful, and exciting than that smaller world I used to live in so contentedly and unquestioningly.

So maybe when we die it's a similar process: another birth. We aren't consulted about the time or manner of our exit, and the process is frightening and uncomfortable, and we don't want to leave the world we know for one that we can't imagine. But, maybe, people who are dying are not the victims of a cruel and senseless fate; they are merely being moved on toward a glorious new life. I'm certainly not certain, but *maybe*!

Maybe death is a transition point instead of a final ending. An introduction to a new phase or stage. A radical change—like when seed pods burst and later become flowers and fruits and vegetables . . . or when food that is eaten turns into energy . . . or when atoms explode and produce power . . . or when ice melts and turns into water . . . or when lava erupts and becomes fertile soil . . . or when trees decay and turn into coal . . . or when rocks are crushed into powder and turn into jewels or into pigments which become, in turn, parts of beautiful paintings.

Maybe there is something real though invisible in us (lots of invisible things are real—love, for instance!) that survives the loss of our bodies and goes to a place we can't yet see.

We don't know whether or not our struggles are going to result in ultimate success that will make them worthwhile, for the simple reason that we haven't yet reached our final destination.

We have to keep going forward into unknown, unexplored territory. Often our experiences en route only seem to make real sense when we can look back on them, not while we are living through them. Later we are able to see that something we considered tragic or pointless or wasteful at the time turned out to be useful and good, because it led to something else or taught us something important, even though we didn't realize it and rebelled against it while it was happening.

Are we like the frightened and mutinous sailors in Columbus' crew who were sure they were heading into nothingness, doomed to disaster and annihilation, when they were actually sailing toward a fascinating "new world"?

All kinds of wrong ideas have been believed throughout history by all kinds of people. But so have some right ideas. So the idea of immortality might be true or it might be false, mere fantasy. The fact that people have, or haven't, believed it cannot give us absolute certainty one way or the other. People who think it's true could be mistaken—but so could people who think it's nonsense.

If it *is* true, I'll have a very happy surprise after I'm dead. If it isn't, I'll never know—because I will have ceased to exist.

So, for the time being, I might as well at least keep open-minded on the subject and *hope*. What can I lose by hoping?

I cannot know, for certain, what happens after death until I myself have experienced death. I cannot know what's behind a closed door until I have opened the door and gone through it.

But I don't have to assume, like an arrogant know-it-all, that I know beyond question that death is the final annihilation of everyone and everything I love. I can't know that, for sure, any more than I can know the opposite.

So let me not stubbornly and pessimistically close my mind to *any* possibility. Let me peacefully wait, until it is the appropriate time for me to find out whatever it is that I am meant to find out—like a child who can't learn to read before it has learned to talk, or to run until it has learned to walk.

Help me to be brave.

Help me to be hopeful.

Help me to face cheerfully and openly—rather than reluctantly and resentfully—whatever is coming next, wherever it is that I am going.

A prayer for the person I love who is dying:

DEAR LORD, welcome this traveler who has roamed the whole world with an eager and observant eye and a responsive heart. Welcome him as he goes forth now on a new journey to an unknown place.

It is always so hard to say goodbye to someone we love, but we are willing to do so if we know the person is embarking on the next stage of a fascinating journey and that he or she is always curious to see things never before seen, happy to voyage to places never before seen, ready to love appreciatively what has never before been known and to rejoice in what is loved. So help me to accept the fact that he is parting from me now, traveling far away from me, and help me to hope that we will be rejoined some day.

His journey in recent months has been hard, and he is tired. You created him and led him from birth through infancy and childhood and maturity to his final destination, so don't desert him now. Comfort him with everlasting love. And also comfort me, who will miss him so very much, and help me to remember, and to share, and to keep alive his spirit of adventure and love of life. Amen!

The sorrow we feel when we lose someone or something we love is the measure of how valuable he or she or it was to us. The pain is slight if the value was small, great if it was great, immeasurable if it was priceless. A loss would be hardly noticeable, let alone painful, if what was lost was worth nothing.

So we would never know suffering if happiness didn't exist! Sorrow is the price we pay for joy. It's the dark shadow cast by bright sunlight.

And is it really so strange or unreasonable that something which is worth an awful lot, and which we enjoy a great deal, should cost us something? We have to pay for a good education, a football game, a theater ticket, delicious food, a beautiful dress, a diamond ring, a home, and we don't resent paying. Why should we resent having to pay a price for things that are worth far more: e.g. happiness, knowledge, love?

Why have I always taken good things for granted and not been more curious about how they got there and why?

And why have I assumed that the existence of bad things outweighed the existence of good things, instead of the other way around?

Death is the absence of life and illness is the absence of health—but life and health are great miracles which we thoughtlessly, foolishly, take for granted until we lose them.

Do I wish I had never known love or happiness because it is such a terrible loss when they are taken away from me?

No! "Better to have loved and lost than never to have loved at all." Even when happiness has been taken away from us we should still be able to say "Thank you" for the fact that we have once had it. Even if all the things I love are impermanent they are so very beautiful and valuable that to have known them at all makes me fortunate. I might never have been born. If so, I would have been spared suffering but I would also have been "spared" much delight!

So please give me strength . . . courage . . . peace . . . a spirit of deep thankfulness . . . a sense of humor . . . a sense of proportion . . . generosity . . . willingness to be adaptable, and flexibility so that I can part with things and people gracefully when the time comes for them to go from me, as well as genuine responsiveness while they are here, so that I welcome good things and people warmly when they come to me and appreciate them with the admiration and gratitude they deserve.

If God exists he is probably as different from me as a painter is from a painting. A painting could never possibly understand the mind of the artist who made it. But if the painting could think, and knew its value and its source, perhaps it would at least want to *thank* the painter for making it!

Me too. I think I ought to want to thank Whoever or Whatever it is that caused me (and the things and the people that I love) to exist, for my (and for their) existence.

Can we make up for things we've done, or failed to do, in the past? No one can undo the past, and the present is the result of everything we've done in the past. And it's so difficult to change habits that we've developed—especially when they are long-standing habits, whether that means doing things or *not* doing things.

I want to end my habit of complaining and worrying, and cultivate a habit of appreciating and hoping.

How? No use making big brave resolutions. Resolutions are so easy to break. I'll just try to be different *today,* and not worry about tomorrow until tomorrow.

5
Wondering
if there
really is
a God
and, if so,
what God's like

What does the word "G-o-d" actually mean? Is it just a little word that someone made up once, thinking that somehow three letters could explain something nobody really understands?

We often use words to identify and talk about things we can't understand. The word "instinct," for instance. That's a label for a mystery, not an explanation of it. It doesn't tell us *how* birds know how to build nests and get food and fly; it just affirms that they do. I guess the word "God" is similar. It's a three-letter synonym for the greatest of all mysteries, the Mystery back of and beyond and above and beneath all other mysteries.

Because God is a great mystery which I cannot possibly fully fathom, I should at least feel *awe* when I think of the word, instead of using it casually as a cuss word when I stub my toe or someone annoys me.

Trying to figure out all the riddles of existence and explain the universe seems like a hopelessly impossible task to me. It gives me a headache! Trying to get such big ideas into my small head is like trying to put the entire ocean into a child's small sandpail . . .

Maybe the opposite approach would work better: Instead of trying to get the whole ocean into my sandpail I should wade into the surf and sink my whole pail into the ocean! Let the waves wash over it and clean it and fill it to the brim and spilling over . . . sink myself in God instead of trying to squeeze God into me, and become filled with as much of God as I can possibly hold while accepting the fact that I'm obviously too small to hold all of God even though he can hold all of me.

But do I dare? Where would the tides carry me?

So many people think it's "obvious" that there's a God. And many, though not *as* many, think it's "obvious" that there isn't.

Either way, how can they be so *sure*? What *seems* obvious is—obviously!—not always true.

People once thought it was obvious that the sun moves while the earth stays still—because "obviously" the sun rises each morning, travels through the sky and then disappears. (They didn't realize that our viewpoint is inevitably distorted by our human limitations and personal perspective, and that it is very hard to stretch one's mind to the point where one can discover "objective truth.")

And people used to think it was "obvious" that the world was flat—because if it were round then, "obviously," people on the "bottom" would fall off! (They didn't know about the law of gravity and how it helps you do the "impossible.")

And people used to think it was "obvious" that the deaf couldn't be taught anything (Aristotle even said they shouldn't be allowed to vote) and that certain races were inherently and permanently inferior to others (and therefore human slavery was justified). Even though Christians say "God is Love" most people throughout history have failed to realize the "obvious" implications of that statement: that God must, and we should, love everybody. (Do most of us underestimate both God's power and God's love?)

I don't know how to evaluate the various reasons why some people do and some people don't believe in God. How can I ever decide whether the believers or the nonbelievers are right? Not only is Truth not always obvious but it isn't something which can be definitively decided by a conference or a poll or majority vote or by a Supreme Court ruling . . . except that, funnily, I guess that's exactly what God is: the *real* Supreme Court! God is whatever-there-is-that-is-supreme-over-everything-else, the Ultimate Authority.

Something must be "supremer" than everything else. And it wouldn't make sense to say that *nothing* is the supreme "something" because "nothing" isn't "something," it's no thing.

In English the term for whatever-the-supreme-some-thing-is is "God." People could have chosen three other letters than "g" and "o" and "d" to designate it. We could refer to it/him as "ABC" or "XYZ" or "A-to-Z" instead (and in fact Christians call Jesus Christ the "Alpha and Omega" for the first and last letters of the Greek alphabet, to indicate that God is whatever-is-first-and-whatever-is-at-the-final-end-of-everything-else).

Step by step, let me see if I can figure out why some people are *sure* there is a God:

Well, there's *one* thing I'm sure of. There is a universe. It exists. We *know* that.

Nothing ever comes from nothing, so there must be something that produced the universe: its Origin, its Cause.... But then what produced that? Was there a Cause of the Cause? And a Cause of the Cause of the Cause?

Well, however far one tries to expand one's concepts of space and time and causality, it is utterly impossible, for creatures who are limited to a small part of space and time as we humans are, to see that far, but *something* must be the underlying initial cause of everything else.

Whatever the Basic Cause of everything is, it must in *some* way contain life (be alive) because life *does* exist and only something living can produce something living. An inkwell can't produce blood (or even ink, for that matter!). A china doll can't give birth to a baby doll. Only life generates life.

Since it would be a terrible mouthful to have to say, every time you wanted to think or talk about "the Life that gives life to everything that lives and that is the ultimate source of everything in existence," someone invented a short word to mean all that. In English that word is God.

Some of the synonyms that people use for God are Eternal Life, the Eternal Being, the Creator, the Father, the Lord, Ultimate Reality, the Essence of Existence, the Source of Life, the Ground of all Being, "I am what is" (or, as the Bible puts it, Yahweh—"I Am Who Am").

If the word "God" means Eternal Life, or Eternal Being, or the Essence of Existence, then by definition God must exist, since life does. To say "God doesn't exist" is meaningless! God can't help existing if *Existence Itself* (wherever it comes from, whatever its highest capability is, whatever its final end is) is what God is.

Therefore asking "Does God exist?" is the same as asking "Does existence exist?"—to which the only rational answer is "obviously"!

The really important question, then, that I have to ask is not "Does God exist?" but *"What is God like?"*

Couldn't "whatever-is-the-basic-cause-of-everything-that-exists" simply be a small germ or sperm or seed of some kind, a once-living *thing* rather than a still-living "Father"?

What makes anyone think they can talk to it (or to him) or that it (or he) can hear them or gives a hoot about them?

God, What and Who are you?

Is it really possible to get to know you?

You may have made me (directly, or very indirectly by making the atoms and genes and chromosomes and hormones and minerals et cetera of which I consist), but do you *know* me in any sense that is meaningful to *me*?

Are you personal enough for me to talk to? Or for you to talk to me? Have you any human traits, or are you something like a supermagnetic field or electrical force or a microbe?

Are you so far superior to me that you could step on me heedlessly, and squash me, the way I might step unconcernedly on an ant?

Is there any real possibility of a truly loving relationship between us?

Couldn't, perhaps, the First-Cause-of-Everything-Else have existed Once Upon a Time, and then have ceased to exist later—just as a human being can give life and then later die? Maybe God existed once, but is now dead—as it was once so fashionable to say.

But if what God is is *Life Itself*, Life's *essence*, then it doesn't make any sense to say that! Every April and every maternity ward prove that life is still very much alive.

Life can't be dead, any more than Beauty can be ugly or Truth can be false or Goodness can be evil or Love can be hate or Heat can be cold. Those are self-contradictions. God is *Isness*, and Isness *is*.

When people worship God they are not just thinking about the *origin* of existence. They are also thinking about its *value* and its *purpose*. They are aspiring to goodness, to an ultimate ideal.

God is more than just our creator, in other words. People who think about him are thinking about the most fundamental and highest aspects of creation all at once: not merely the First Thing but also the Best Thing and the Final Thing, the *Whole*: origin, process, and goal.

So the word "God" means not just our Maker but "whatever is first and whatever is best *and* whatever is final." Or, to put it another way: the beginning of, the greatest potentiality of, and the ultimate destination of everything that exists.

What makes people think that the First and Best and Last Things are all wrapped up together in one cosmic Being? Couldn't the First Cause of the universe be something quite different and separate from the Best Thing or the Last Thing?

I guess not . . . because the *first* and the *best* and the *last* are all three inherently, inevitably, inextricably, eternally linked by the very fact that the first is the cause of whatever is best and whatever is last . . . and the best is, by definition, the highest result of whatever potential exists within the first . . . and the last is, inevitably, the ultimate fulfillment and destiny of both, of everything.

So the very, very First Being must *contain* the Best and Final Beings within itself, in a mysterious but essential way, and must also be contained within them.

When you really think *hard* about something, you usually begin to understand more about it than you did before, so I'm really trying hard to think hard about God! Here goes:

1. Nobody can give what one doesn't have. So whatever gave existence its qualities must, in some way, possess them.

2. Among the many things that exist are creativity, love, beauty, intelligence—so in some way the Source of these qualities (alias God) must be creative, loving, beautiful, and intelligent.

3. Therefore, God *must* be, in *some* way, *personal*, because these are qualities that are characteristics of persons, not of mere "things."

4. So God is a he—or a she or a he/she or a they—rather than just an it. More than a human being, not less than—more powerful, longer-lived, with a tremendously (infinitely?) greater perspective than the entire human race has, let alone any one human being.

5. If our attitudes weren't limited by our very small egocentric view of things, I guess we'd admire God more than anyone in the whole world!

I guess I see why the word "it" seems too insignificant to describe God. But why do we say "he" instead of "she" or "he/she" or "they"? Maybe it's just a long-standing verbal habit related to the idea that males are superior to females, stronger and smarter and all the rest, and that a ruler or provider is usually masculine.

The myths which the world's very earliest, primitive philosophers developed in their efforts to comprehend and explain the origin of things involved pregnant "mother goddesses," because it seemed self-evident that *mothers* are the source of life. But later, when knowledge of biology developed, people got more sophisticated and realized that the *father* plays a vital role in creating life, and in fact they then thought of the father as life's beginner, begetter, initiator—so it made sense to think of God, the initiator of all life, as a he. But now we realize that *life is produced by an act of love between equal partners*; it's the *union* between them that causes life to begin. So perhaps we should speak of our "Father-Mother God" as the Christian Scientists do—though that sounds a bit strange.

Perhaps it's just that human language is a clumsy instrument. We speak of "man" meaning the human race, though we realize humanity includes woman too, and we say "Mankind" when we probably should say "Man-WomanChildkind."

God, if he-she-it made everyone and everything, must contain in some seminal, fertile way elements of everyone and everything and not be limited by any such factors as sex or age or race or species. If God made *all* things God contains within himself, somehow, *all* potentialities.

Perhaps the best way to solve this gender dilemma is just to forget about saying "him" and say "God"—or better still, to talk *to* instead of *about* God and say "you."

God, if you possess intelligence and intention and are active and conscious, then you are not just a vague abstraction. You have *personal* qualities in some mysterious way—though I'm sure you're not an Old Man With a Beard sitting on a golden throne somewhere high above the clouds, listening to choirs of angels pluck harps and sing your praises or watching cherubs fly around playing ring-toss with their halos. (The symbols used by artists may be charming, but they are as limited and clumsy and inaccurate as the symbols we use in speech.)

You are *above* the human race—not in a geographical "up there" or "out there somewhere" sense, but in the sense that you existed before it did, and are greater than it is, and brought it into existence.

And yet you are also *in* the human race somehow—as the instigator and inspirer of our highest ideals and deepest longings and most loving deeds and greatest wisdom, as our "life force" and the creativity that underlies and permeates our own creativity.

You are alive in us *and* alive independently of us *and* you are the living link between what is within and what is beyond us.

Trying to figure out what God is like means trying to figure out what kind of "thing" could possibly, all at once, *create* life, *sustain* life, and *fulfill* life.

There is only *one* thing I can think of which answers that description:

Love!

And that's what the Bible says God is.

What is the creative process? What basic motive, power, or inspiration must a creator possess? By understanding that, perhaps one can get to understand *the* Creator?

Hate isn't a creative force—on the contrary, it's destructive. Indifference isn't creative, either—it's paralyzing. And egotism isn't creative—it produces ingrown isolation and sterility, not outgoing activity.

What *is* creative? *Love.*

Creation is an act of love: great or small, complete or partial, physical or mental. Cute babies, delicious meals, pretty clothes, good conversations, impressive theatrical productions, art exhibits, gorgeous concerts . . . all are produced by varying types and degrees of love.

Love is the one motive or power there is which is truly productive, constructive, sustaining, and enriching— every kind of love (i.e., attraction and urge toward union), from the mechanical and chemical up to and through the intellectual and spiritual on an ascending ladder. Plants grow by turning to and reaching up for the sun. Bees are fed as a result of their love of honey. Gardens bloom because gardeners love and care for flowers. Cubs thrive when protected by loving mother bears. Paintings emerge out of artists' love of forms and colors. Music is created because composers love sounds and rhythms. Books are written because writers love words and ideas. Pupils learn because teachers love them and love the subjects they teach. Families prosper and are made happy when love flows between their members.

So maybe the old song is right when it says that love actually is what makes the world go around! Dante prayed to "the Love that moves the sun and the stars." If Love is the "life force" then Love is the nature of life's creator.

If God originates, protects, and fulfills all creation, then God is:

> not just a clever inventor or manufacturer or great watchmaker

> not just a celestial traffic cop or mighty ruler or king

> not just a scary, stern, universal judge

> not a philosophical proposition or hypothesis or mathematical equation

> not a primal blob of protoplasm or an electronic particle or a prototype of DNA

> not a cold, impersonal, mindless thing

> not an invention of imaginative people
> (it's the other way around!)

God is Love! Active, Productive, Life-giving, Protective, Nourishing, Forgiving, Enriching, Undying, Limitless *Love.*

In the history of the universe, Love is the ultimate source, the power which makes and preserves us. (In short—the Creator.)

In the history of the human race, Love is the main characteristic of the best example of humanity, and the essence of the way in which all humans should live to achieve peace and happiness and to conquer evil. (In short, our Teacher and Savior.)

In the history of each individual human life, Love is the inspiration which, if we follow it, leads us to and unites us with our Creator and our Savior and each other. (In short, our Comforter and Sanctifier.)

So that's why Christians call God a "Trinity" (which means three-in-one). "Trinity" doesn't mean there are three Gods or that God is a three-headed freak, but simply that there are three dimensions or three basic relationships through which God (Love) is revealed to us:

1. The "Father," Creative Love, is the initiative which brings forth life and nourishes and sustains it.

2. The "Son," Redeeming Love, is the example which shows us the way by which we can be saved from the tragic and hideous results of lovelessness (sin).

3. The "Holy Spirit," Sanctifying Love, is the inspiration which guides us and unites us to Creative and Redeeming Love.

But can it really be true that Love is what God is? *Love* made and rules the universe? It certainly doesn't seem so, when you look around and see animals and people killing each other all over the place! (But the funny thing is that even there love is the original motivating force: animals kill because they love food and survival and their offspring; some men kill because they love their country or ideology or property. Hate and fear, anger and cruelty, selfishness and destructiveness become involved, but the primary impelling motive of all action is some kind of love.)

What on earth, or in heaven, am I talking about? What *is* love, anyway? Every enthusiast uses that word to describe good feelings about everything from spaghetti to romance and beyond!

Has the love of a movie fan for a glamorous star got anything in common with a child's love for a favorite toy, a glutton's love of food, a plant's love of sunlight, a wife's love for a husband, a saint's love of God, or God's love for us?

Yes! In every case, love means being drawn toward the object that is loved, in order to merge with or possess it. It's being attracted to what is loved, having a strong urge to be close to and united with it.

And love can't exist without giving something as well as receiving something, even if all the lover can give is yearning or praise. A child gives a toy admiration or concentration, a fan gives a movie star worship, nothing more, but they'd give more if they could. Love is caring and wanting to share. It's aspiring toward and offering to, as well as getting pleasure and warmth from. It's both active and responsive, benefiting and being benefited by, giving and receiving.

And *giving-and-receiving is what life is all about.* The whole universe is a vast complex system of interrelationships in which everything is united in some way, giving something to and receiving something from everything else: minerals, plants, and animals give their very existence to make other existence possible.

If giving-and-receiving is what life is about and if that is what love basically is, then Love is *truly*, not just metaphorically, the most fundamental characteristic of the universe, the one ultimate necessity of life (which is another way of saying that God is Love, and vice versa).

It's really fascinating to think about this, and to realize that some form of love is in operation when *any* form of existence comes into being and is kept in existence.

Another amazing thought: Love is not only the most essential, the most beneficial, the most beautiful thing in the universe, it is also absolutely *unique*—the only thing there is that can be given away without ever diminishing the giver. The more love one gives the more oneself is enriched: A lover still possesses the love he gives away. . . . So if God is Love, God is endless, and indestructible! In other words, infinite and eternal.

I love babies. I think it's absolutely fantastic and marvelous that the result of an act of passionate love between two people can be a whole new human being.

So I have to admit this much. If "Creative Love" is what the word "God" means, I love God!

I love seashells. And flowers. And birds. And animals. I think it is utterly astounding that shapes and colors and textures should exist that are so varied and so incredibly beautiful. And I don't think it can be sheer chance that feathers and petals and features so *consistently* appear in such intricate and lovely designs. Nature is far too complex and too prolific for these similarities to pop up entirely accidentally.

So I have to admit that whatever power it is that can design and produce so much beauty is worthy of my awed appreciation. If the name for that power is God, I love God!

I love the sea and the sky. The sun, the moon, and the stars. Rain, wind, snow. The sounds, smells, sight, taste, touch of so many things! Grass, trees, wild flowers. White beaches and sea gulls, sculptured sand dunes, surf, and rocks. Sunlight glistening on a lake, white caps on the ocean. Murmuring brooks, mist, fog, clouds. Wind blowing across a wheat field, bowing down the grain. Mountains and valleys. Icicles. Leaping flames. Stately pine trees. Zinnias and hyacinths. Puppies' soft floppy ears and cold noses. Kittens' whiskers. Birds' feathers, birds' songs. Oh, the list could go on and on!

I also love the beautiful things that people make: sculpture, painting, photography, books, music, architecture, drama, poetry.

In short, I love beauty in all its varied forms. I rejoice that it exists and that I, too, have been allowed to exist so that I could experience an awareness of it. . . . I shouldn't take it for granted because it is glorious.

Yes, there are many, many things in the universe that owe their existence to something which has not only marvelous, amazing power, but Glory!

For this wonderful fact I give thanks—from the very bottom of my heart.

God, why haven't you made me know and love you before this, if that's what I'm supposed to do?

I guess you couldn't, because you can't be inconsistent. You can't give us liberty to decide for ourselves what we want to do and at the same time make our decisions for us. You may be the Ruler of the universe but you don't rule by bullying or dictating; you delegate control to us where it affects us. You present us with tools and guidelines and inspiration and goals but you don't *compel* us to do anything, because you respect our freedom and individuality.

The Bible says that God made us in his image. This doesn't mean that if we look in a mirror we will see what you look like and that you have a nose, mouth, and chin, two eyes and two ears, etc. It means that you have given us some of your own qualities, including the power to know, love, and create—not totally or perfectly, because we're finite, but enough to affect our lives and the world in a real way. You may be "all-powerful" but you *share* your power with us instead of hogging it all for yourself. So we are free to love you or reject you.

The Bible also says that God is Love. If this is true, as I think I'm beginning to see, you *can't* force your way into us—because true love *never* violates the freedom of another. A lover wants to be loved in return but knows the difference between rape and a real act of love. Love *has* to be given freely or it isn't love. You want us to love you but you want us to *mean* it because we want it. You don't want us to submit because we have to.

So I can't cop out and try to force you to force me to get to know and love you! I can keep your love from entering my heart, and I can deny you mine. You respect my right to choose. How close I get to you is up to *me*. To experience your love fully I have to offer you mine, fully and voluntarily.

6
Hoping to
learn more
and to
find peace,
even joy

Okay, God—let's be friends.

Now . . . if I want to be your friend and have you be mine, that means I am going to have to (no! *want* to) spend a little time alone with you regularly.

Why?

Because friends don't avoid and neglect each other; they want to be in each other's company, to be together and talk things over.

I'll have to be willing to take time out from work and distractions to be with you now and then and to talk with you, honestly and unselfconsciously, and also to keep quiet sometimes and *listen* to you—I mustn't monopolize the conversation!

But you don't speak in the way other people do. How can I hear you? How can I get your message if you have one for me?

By increasing my awareness of your best gifts, becoming more sensitive to them, and by staying in conscious contact with that aspect of you that is contained in my own best self?

I would like to believe whatever is truly true (rather than be deluded), just as I would like to be able to admire anything that is truly admirable and love what is truly lovely (rather than have such bad taste that I prefer things which are cheap or ugly, or be so warped emotionally that I love things which are perverse and hateful).

In short, I'd like to make sense, and to have *appropriate* reactions, and to be appreciative of good and true things.

I promise to try to do my best to look for truth and beauty and goodness, wherever they are, and to try to respond to them with grateful, observant, attentive love.

I would like to be among the people who not only recognize and value true and beautiful and good things, but also one of those who *add* to the world's beauty and goodness instead of being one of the thoughtless or vicious people who neglect, or harm, or destroy good things and people.

This means that I want to **unite** myself to whatever exists that is good and beautiful and true, and turn myself away from whatever is bad and ugly, hateful and false.

If God is the shorthand term, or the nickname, of good-ness-and-beauty-and-truth-and-love, then God is what/who I want to be close to and one with.

How do I do that?

By deciding to!

No matter how much, in the past, I may have ignored or harmed or neglected goodness-beauty-truth-love, as long as I am alive I will have new opportunities to change, to improve, to deepen my appreciation and understanding.

That's what I would like to do during the rest of my life—not just benefit occasionally from goodness and beauty and truth and love, but make a point of *dwelling* on these things, "getting with it," "putting it all together."

I can't help being a happier and better person if I think on such things, instead of brooding bitterly or perplexedly or exaggeratedly on their opposites.

But isn't this pretty theoretical? Can I really expect ever to be happy again after I've lost my heart's desire, the person I love more than the whole rest of the world put together? Talking about the existence of love in general seems vague and abstract, cold comfort.

Well, we'll see. I'll try to *enlarge* my heart and my understanding. I must keep reminding myself that *the whole is greater than any of its parts* and that to love any one part more than the whole is to misplace one's heart and distort one's emotions. It's idolatry, in fact, and that's wrong—not because a scowling, jealous God is going to get his feelings hurt and scold me for it, but because it's inherently illogical and disproportionate and therefore self-defeatingly foolish. I must realize that whatever I love about the things and people I love exists in other expressions and forms too, even when a particular example is no longer visible to me. I must learn to *merge* (though not *sub*merge) my personal concerns in others. I can't, and shouldn't, deny the value of my very important-to-me personal love but I can *add* to it.

If I can really teach myself to unite myself with every-thing-good-that-is then I can never feel isolated and deserted. If I can really learn to *feel* that everything worth loving is part of me and that I am part of everything worth loving, then no individual loss can leave me totally bereft and inconsolable because there will always be other lovely things with which I am intimately involved.

It's important to keep one's values straight. It's so easy to forget how good goodness is or how beautiful beauty is if we concentrate on their opposites (like the newspaper editors who think that only bad news is news, and who make us all think there never is any important good news). So *every day* I should pause for a little while to think about good and lovely things.

This wouldn't be silly or a waste of time. It would be like taking vitamin pills regularly to keep well—or sleeping peacefully every night in order to restore energy for activity the next day.

It might lead to a more consistently grateful heart, a more cheerful disposition, a more peaceful spirit—while concentrating on the opposite means cultivating, increasing, and wallowing in fear and hatred and anger and depression.

Here is a prayer I guess I can honestly utter, even when I'm unhappy:

Thank you—whoever you are who is the source of everything beautiful and good and lovely that I have ever loved, you who are the Beauty that gives itself to beautiful things, and the Goodness that is within everything good, and the Loveliness that makes lovely whatever is lovely. Thank you for letting me live, so that I could experience and share some of your beauty and goodness.

Aside from sitting quietly now and then, thinking about you, I guess I should also read some of the things written by other people who have thought a lot about you and talked to you, and find out what they think they have learned.

I suppose I could start by reading the Bible—in a modern version that I can understand, because it's too easy to become confused and even misled by an archaic vocabulary. I won't be reading it in order to appreciate beautiful poetry but to try to get at the *meaning*.

Do I have to read through both the Hebrew and the Christian scriptures and the Bhagavad-Gita and the works of Buddha's disciples and all the other writings of the world's saints and religious thinkers? I'll never make it!

But I should read *some* things—and not just with my eyes but with my mind and my heart wide open, *thinking* and *praying* about what I read, and *applying* what I learn.

Why should I read the Bible? Well, for one thing, to find out why the personality and message of Christ have attracted and moved so many people so tremendously for so many centuries, inspiring both bright and stupid, good and bad, educated and ignorant, sophisticated and naïve, saintly and sinful people so very much.

He had no press agents, money, newspaper publicity, nor TV exposure, no powerful friends nor big political machine working for him, yet he has had enormous influence on millions and millions of people all over the globe. He lived a short life in a small town in a small colony of an empire that collapsed a long time ago, yet he not only became world-famous, but still is more than twenty centuries after his death. So many generations have come and gone since he died, opinions and philosophies and tastes and customs and institutions have all undergone huge unforeseeable changes, and so many new things have been invented and discovered—yet people still pay attention to this man's words and example, and think they are still relevant.

How come?

So many people think he is the best guide there is, ever was, or ever will be to happiness and goodness. It's therefore not fair—to truth, or to him, or to myself—for me to ignore him.

But Christ didn't seem to think you have to be a great scholar or intellectual to make friends with God—thank God! He said we should be like little children, and little children can't read *anything*, let alone weighty tomes by philosophers and theologians and historians.

What did Christ mean, I wonder, when he said we should be like small children? Surely he wasn't recommending ignorance and temper tantrums and grabbing each other's toys and all the other exasperating things small children do. I guess he meant:

> Realize that you don't, and can't, know everything, but be curious and eager to learn as much as you can (children are always asking "why?" and "what's that?").

> Be grateful for what you have, especially for love (babies always "love back" anyone who is good to them, no matter how poor or funny-looking they are).

> Be trusting (little children believe what they're told; also they know they can't take care of themselves, so they rely on other people and don't mind having to).

> Ask for what you need, without pride or embarrassment (babies squawk determinedly when they need something).

Oh God, you who brought me, without consulting me, without my knowledge of what you were doing or why, into this difficult and puzzling but also fascinating world, help me to trust you to know what you're doing.

I owe every single thing I have, and am, and know, and enjoy, and love, to your generosity, initiative, intelligence, and power . . . all summed up in the all-encompassing phrase "creative love." So why shouldn't I trust you? Because you give us things we love and then take them away, which is cruel? But even if that's the way things work, it's not entirely cruel—because sharing and lending are better than never giving anyone anything at all. And maybe you give things back again later, after you've taken them away, or replace them with better things—the way maturity follows childhood and daytime follows night and spring follows winter.

Teach me to be trusting, instead of cynical; peaceful, instead of quarrelsome; humble, instead of arrogant. Teach me to stop thinking I know more and better than the Being that gave me my being!

You are powerful enough to create things as huge as continents, and even bigger things like stars and solar systems, and even vaster things like galaxies and—at the very same time—things as tiny as ladybugs, and pores in the skin, and even tinier atoms, and even more infinitesimal electronic particles. So you are obviously not bothered by the size of a task!

You are evidently capable of paying attention to many, many things at once, designing and producing and distributing an infinity of unique fingerprints and snowflakes even while you are juggling groups of planets in the air. Your eye for precision and detail enables you to keep on turning out peacock feathers and inchworms and four-leaf clovers in the same instant that you are controlling the tides and guiding comets thousands of light years away on split-second schedules.

So, in a way, it seems sort of silly for me to think you can't guide me! I am neither the very smallest nor the very biggest, the least or the most important or complicated thing in your universe—and I belong here just as surely as the Himalayas or a wild flower that you have planted by a brook. So you can guide me if I'll let you!

I *WILL* let you!

Teach me to accept the fact that it is impossible for me to understand everything—in other words, you—because I am finite. Teach me to accept my limitations peacefully.

And teach me not to close mental doors on increased understanding—because, even if I can never know everything, I can always learn more than I now know.

So let me not become dogmatic and cocksure, narrow, opinionated, or stubborn. When you lead me toward a new experience and added knowledge, don't let me pull back and refuse to go where you are leading me or refuse to look at what you are trying to show me.

Remind me not to be hostile, or resentful, or fearful of the truth, whatever the truth is.

Words, words, words!

They seem so repetitious and so inadequate. It's so hard to express one's deepest thoughts and loves and fears and hopes in words. And each of us, in a fundamental way, is to some extent so unknown—to other people and even to ourselves.

No book of prayers composed by someone else could ever fully answer my needs. Even prayers composed by me couldn't fully, always, say what I want to say and what I need to say.

There are times when I am going to have to go beyond words if I am going to try to contact God and stay in contact. Sometimes I should silence my heart in order to listen, and let God do the talking.

If I am truly serious about wanting to hear what you have to teach me, I must—at times—suspend my own internal and external chatter.

Silence can be an empty void caused by the hollowness of inactivity, of nothingness, of death. That's certainly not what I'm after. It can also be a boring intermission between activities, or a salutary, pleasant rest and cure when one is tired. Those are not what I want, either.

The kind of silence I want to cultivate is spacious and creative—the quiet peace which encourages slow but steady growth, as within a womb or a seed pod. The silence of unanxious but alert expectancy, as when you are waiting for a knock on the door from someone you love, or an important telephone call. An unargumentative awareness, patient yet eager—so that I won't miss my cue if you give me one.

God: Teach me to let my soul rest, to still my worries and doubts, to stop my constant chatter of questions and protests.

Let me come to you sometimes and just sit quietly, like a mother smiling at her sleeping baby and listening to its soft breathing . . . or like a small child intent on hearing a kitten's purr or a little bird's chirp . . . or as if I were trying to hear a soft breeze moving across a pond, or a leaf dropping onto the grass.

Let me learn to wait patiently and trustingly for you to make things clearer to me.

Teach me to be as calm as a lake after sundown . . . as trusting as a baby in its mother's lap. Teach me to grow gradually, unprotestingly, like a flower . . . to go un-resistingly wherever you send me, like an airborne seed obeying the breeze. Teach me to turn always toward you, the very essence of love and of life, the cause of love and life, the nourisher of love and life, the purpose of love and life—the way leaves keep turning toward the life-giving sun.

In spite of all the many things I don't understand,
in spite of all the many things I don't like,
in spite of all that I wish I had and don't have,
in spite of all that I do have and wish I didn't have,
in spite of joys I have lost and suffering I have found,
     thank you, God.

For all the good things I do have and
for all the good things I have had and
for all the good things I will have,
for what I am,
for what I have been,
for what I can be,
for what I shall be,
     thank you, God.

For flowers,
for seashells,
for art,
for music,
for birds,
for dogs,
for ducks,
for geese,
for water,
for air,
for sky,
for stars,
for sunshine,
for earth,
for grass,
for food,
for drink,
for laughter,
for affection,
for my friends,
for my family,
for my parents,
for my children,
for my beloved husband,
for my life,
thank you, God . . . even if it's all only a loan.

Thank you for *all* the beautiful things in the world and in the universe—and in universes beyond this universe, if there are any!

Thank you for all the good things I know about, and for the inexhaustible supply of those that I haven't discovered yet. And remind me to keep searching and to continue noticing.

Thank you for all the things I love that I can see and hear and touch and taste and smell. And also for all the invisible and intangible things that have no physical shape or sound or texture or flavor or odor but which are equally real just the same and which make life so lovely wherever they are found—such things as:

true friendship
loyalty
kindness
understanding
tenderness
generosity
patience
courage
creativity
imagination
hope
faith

and above all, thank you for *love*, which includes and sums up all those qualities.

And thank you for the even more basic essences, the abstract qualities that are the underlying, invisible, universal "soul" of these qualities:

beauty itself
goodness itself
truth itself
existence itself

In short, God:
    thank you for being,
    thank you for Being,
    thank you for Being You.

THANK YOU!